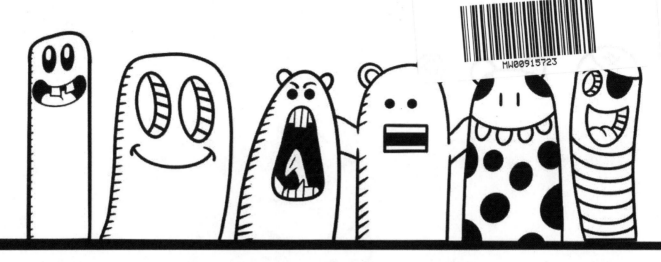

THIS BOOK BELONGS TO

Thank You!

DRAWN BY MOUTH BY QUADRIPLEGIC
MOUTH ARTIST ~ ANDREW EVANS.

WATCH ME DRAW THIS COVER,
➤➤ YOUTUBE - SMART MOUTH ART ◄◄

Smart Mouth Art
DRAWN BY MOUTH

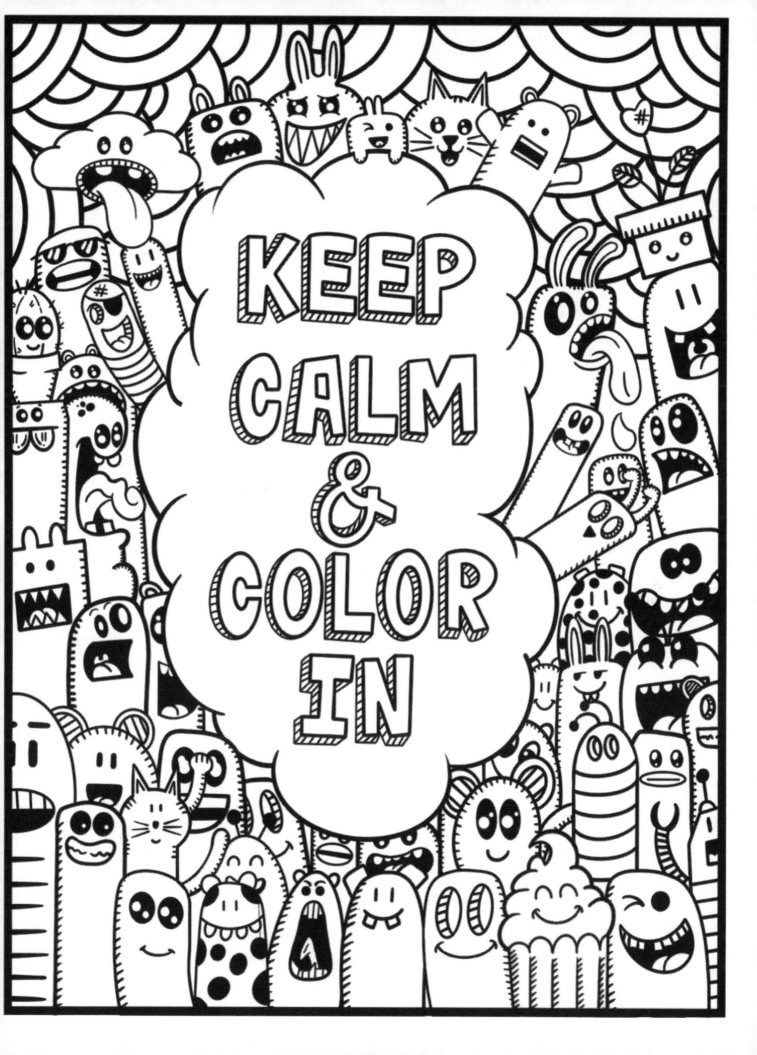

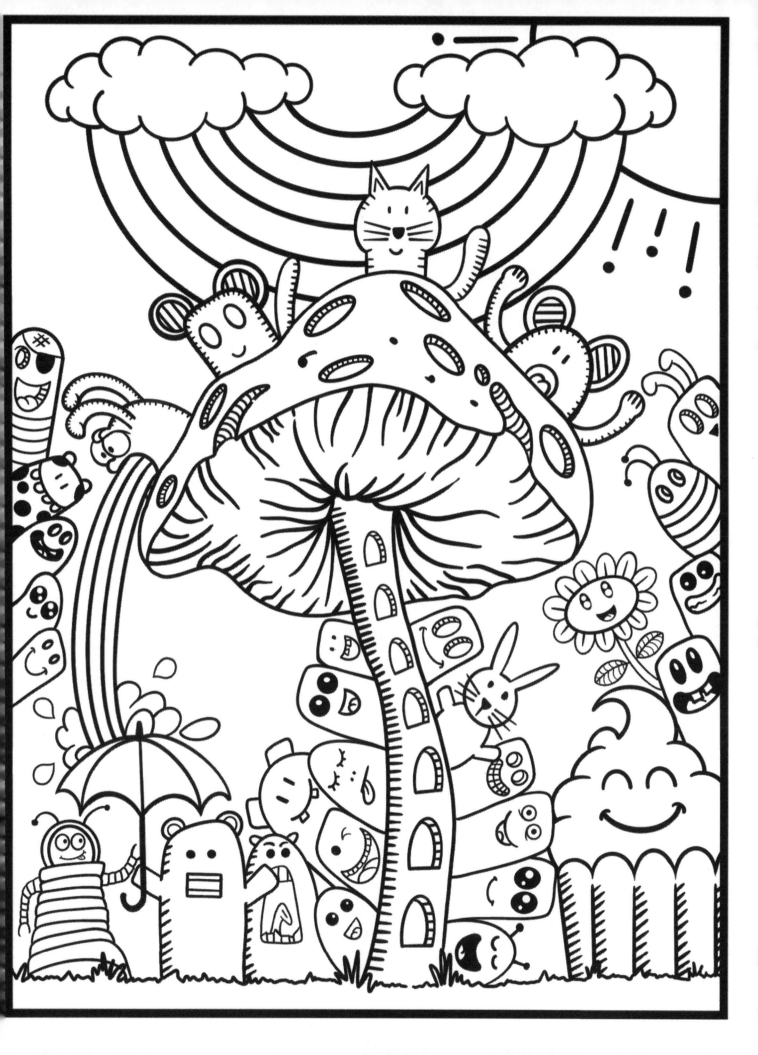

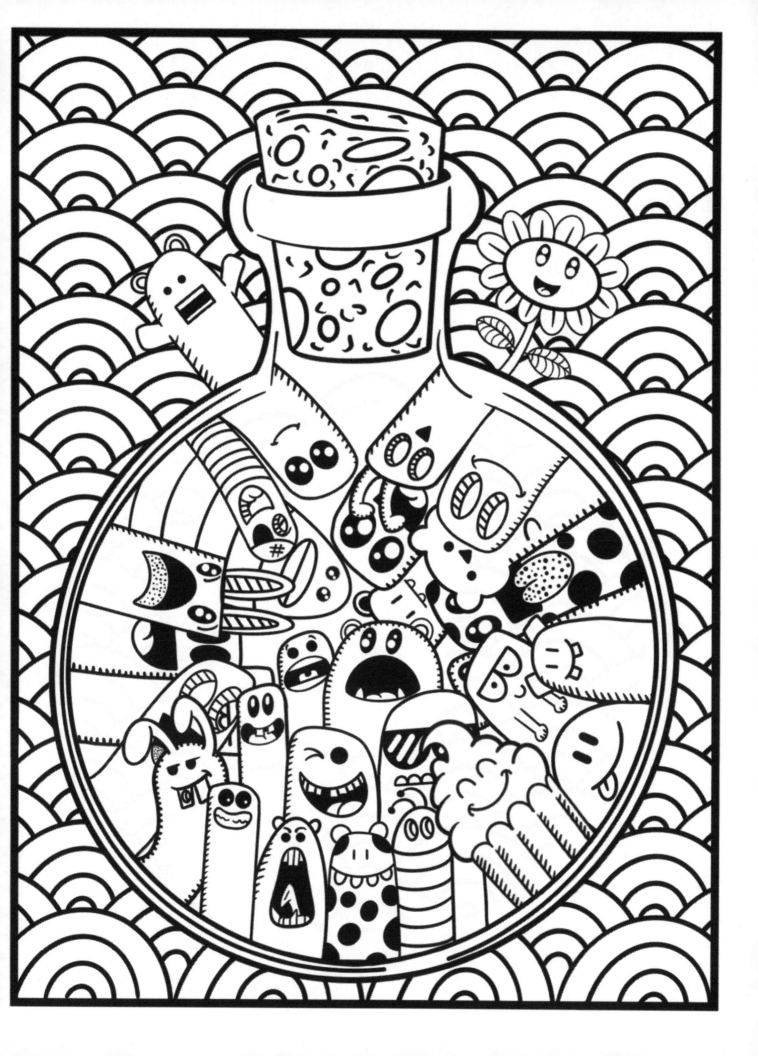

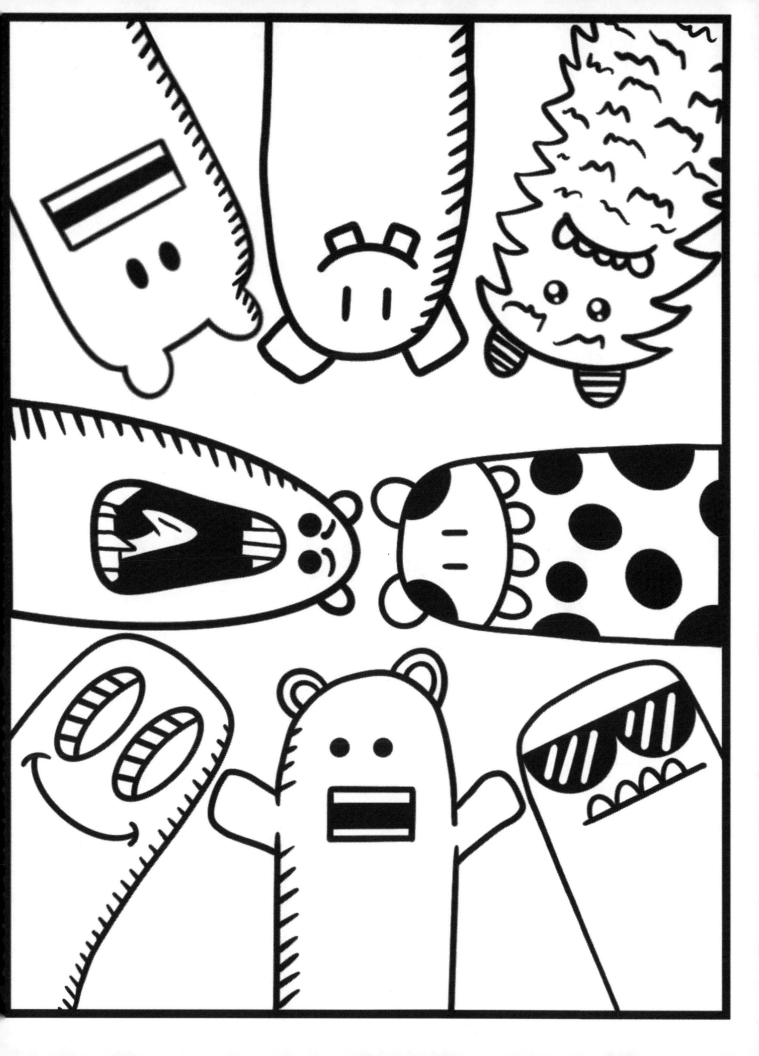

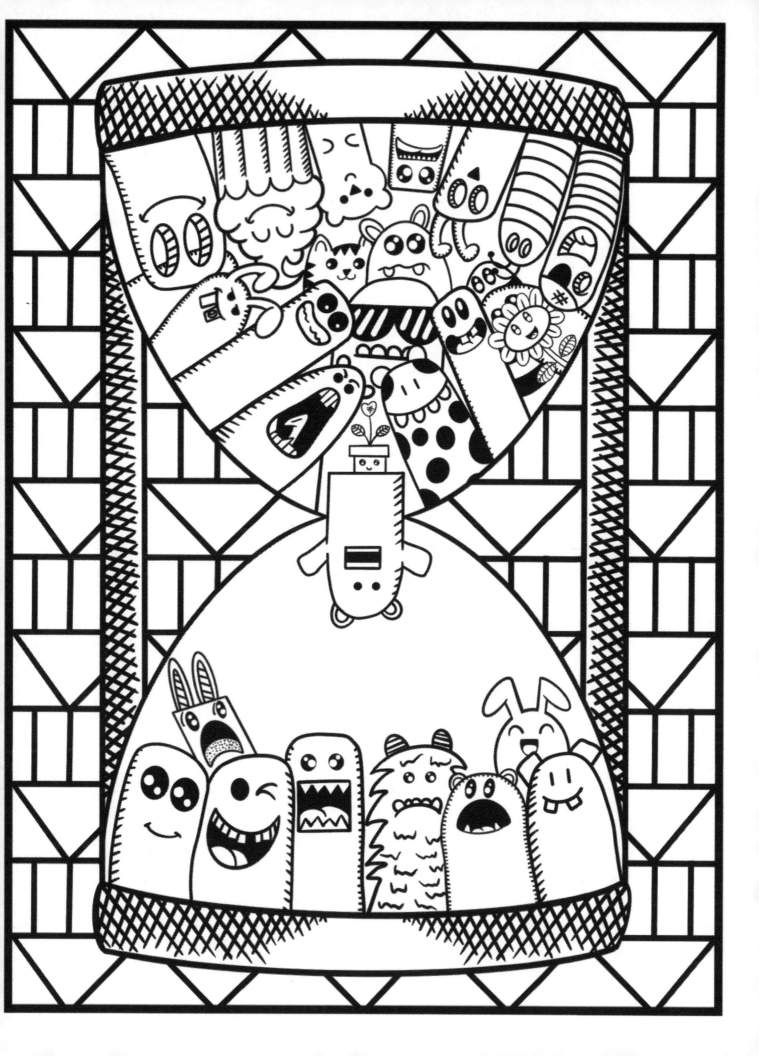

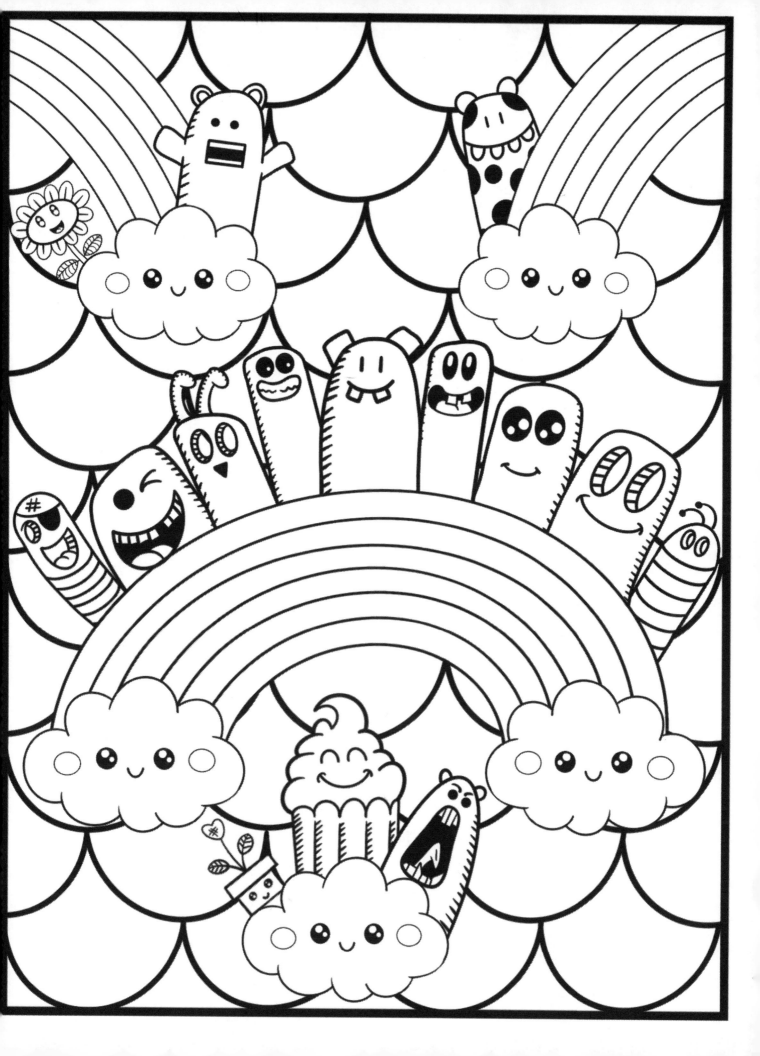

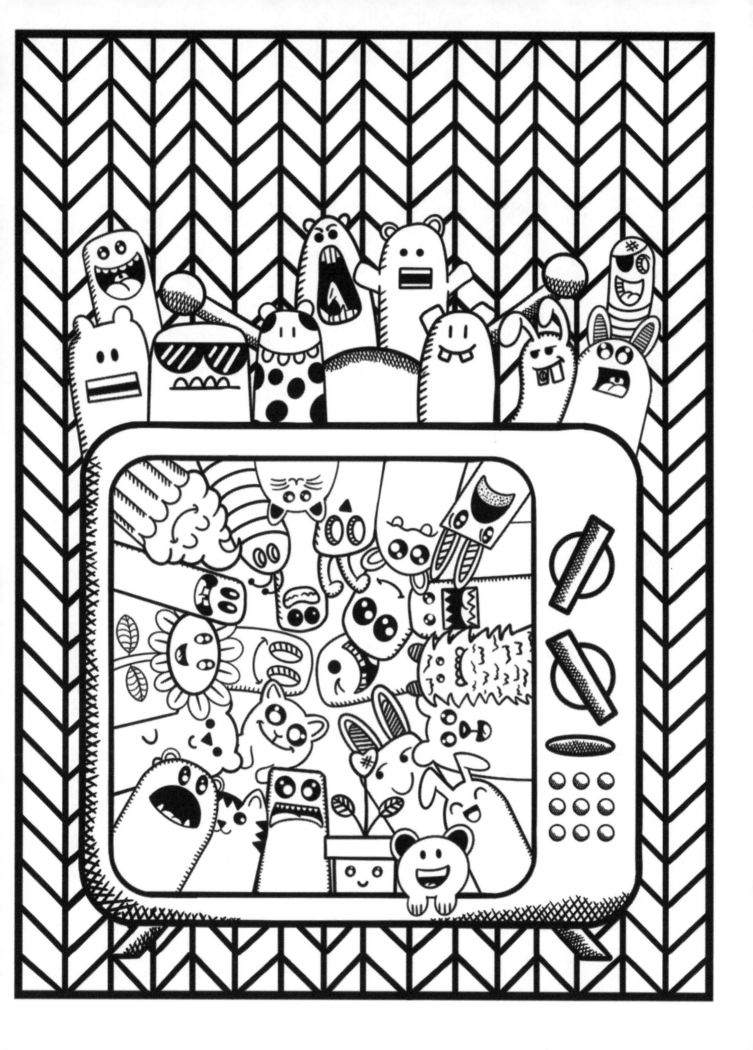

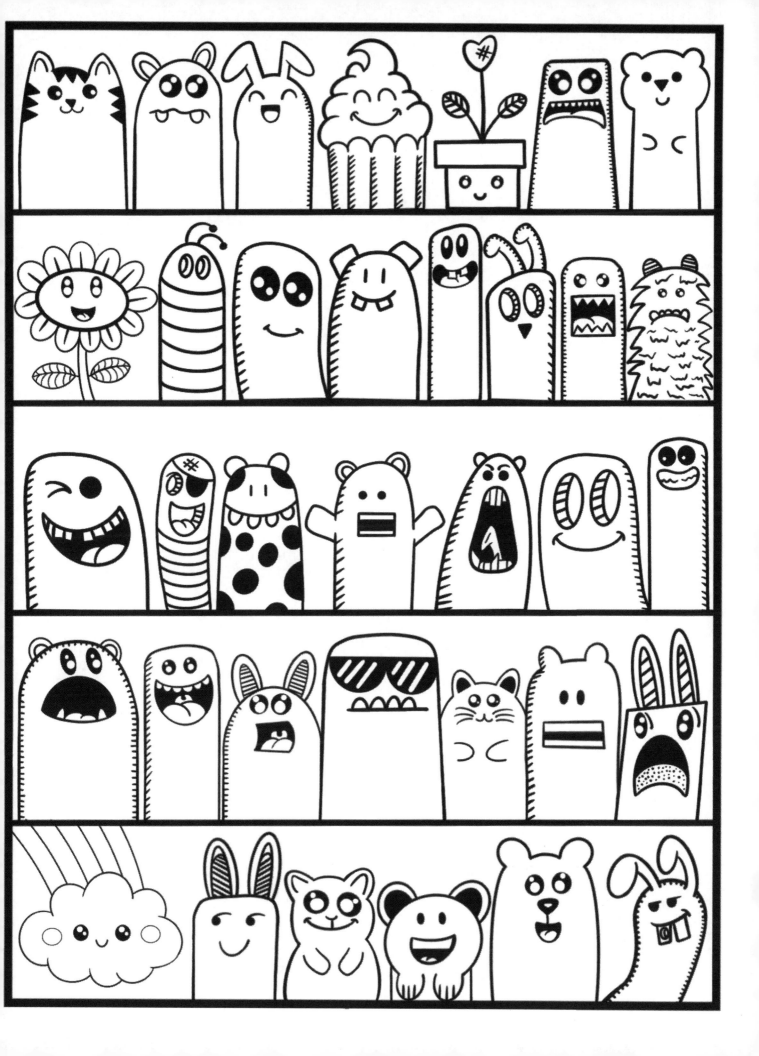

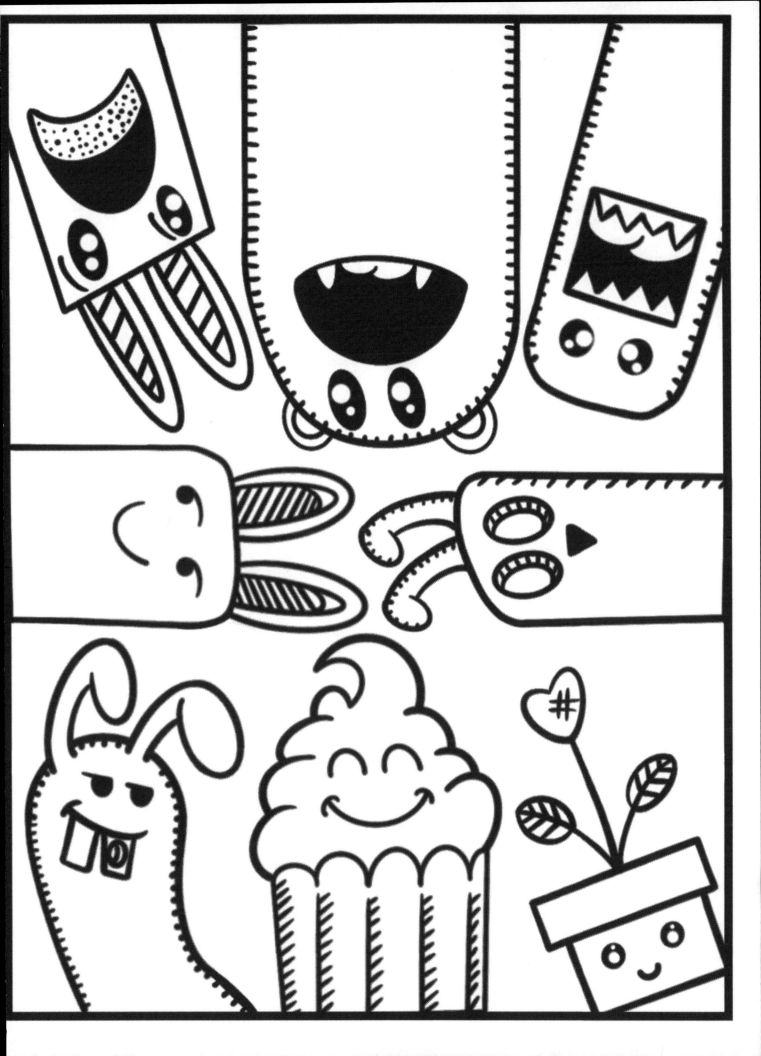

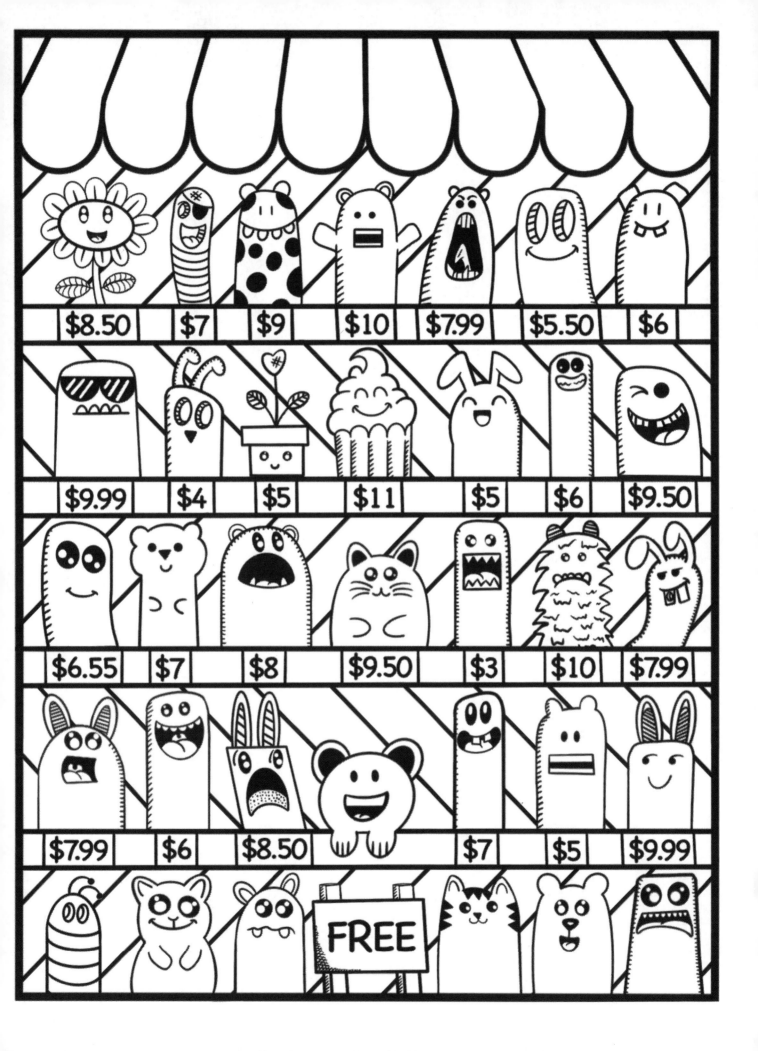

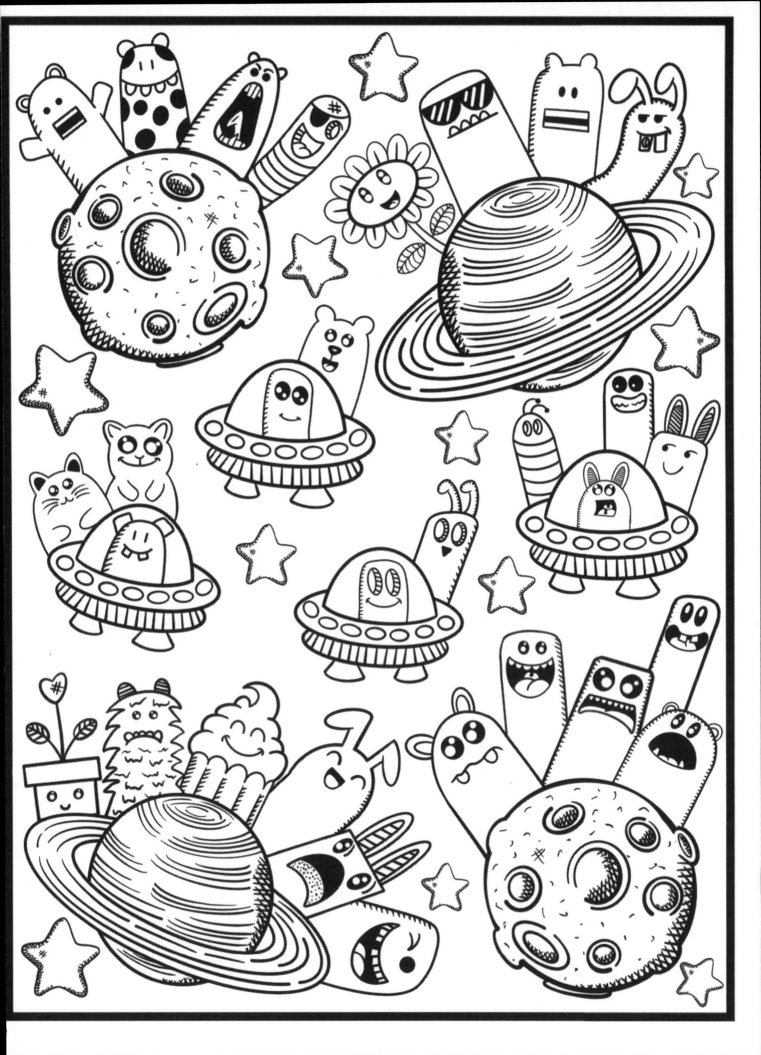

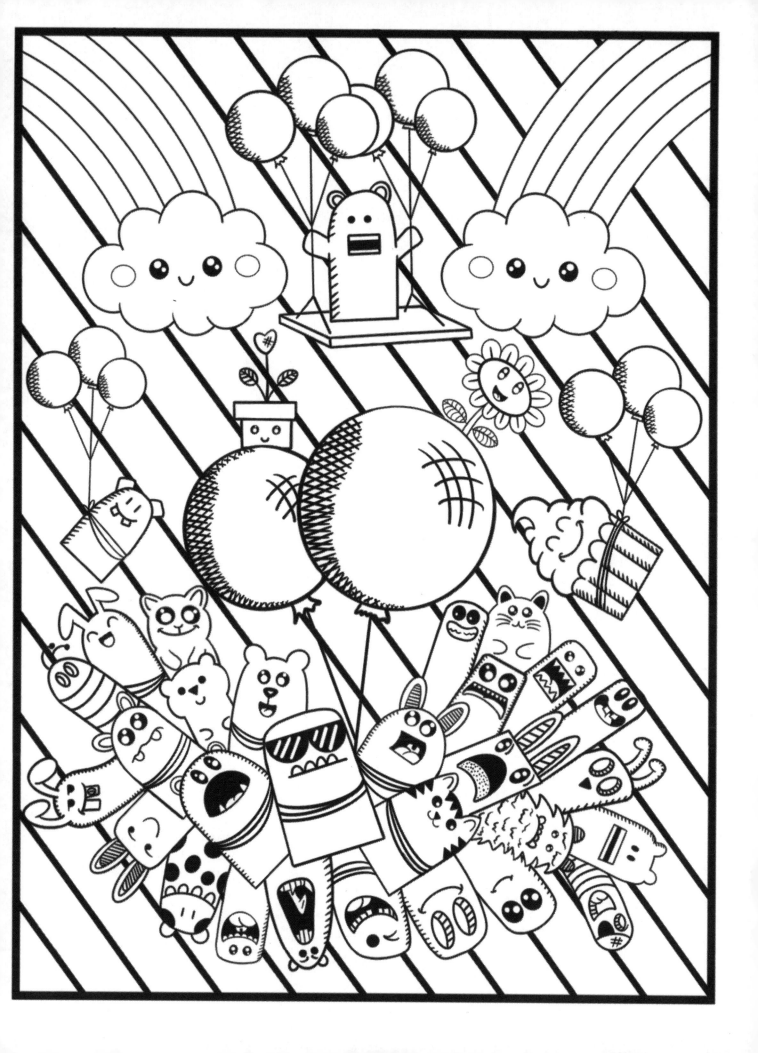

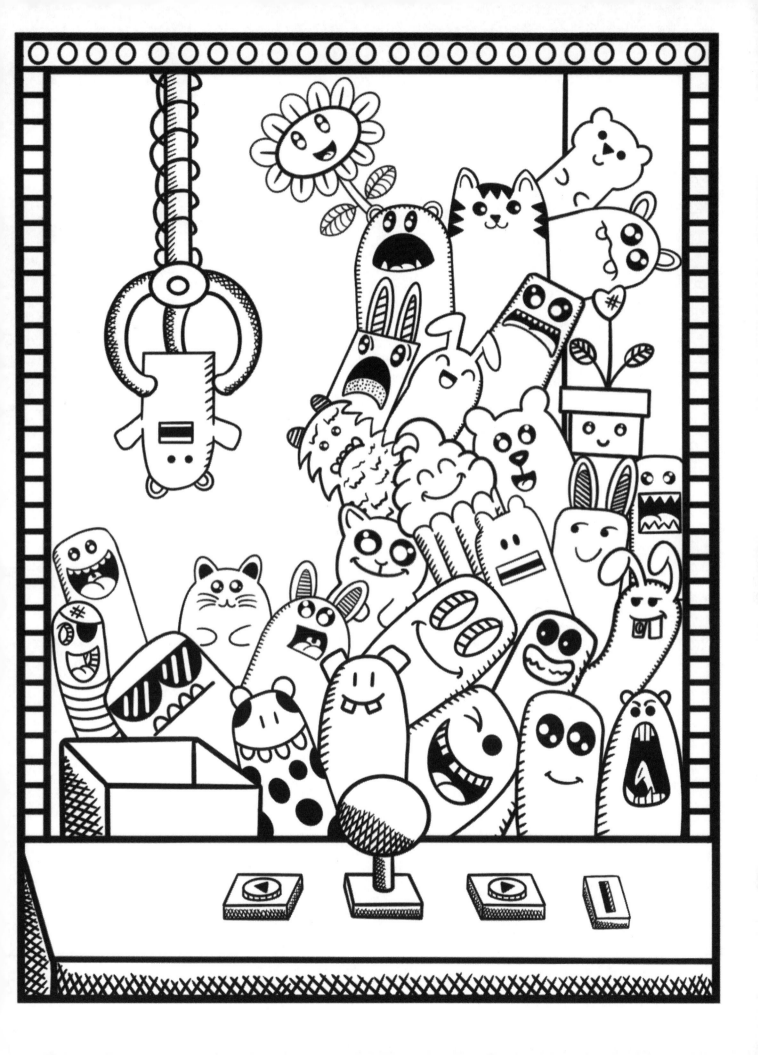

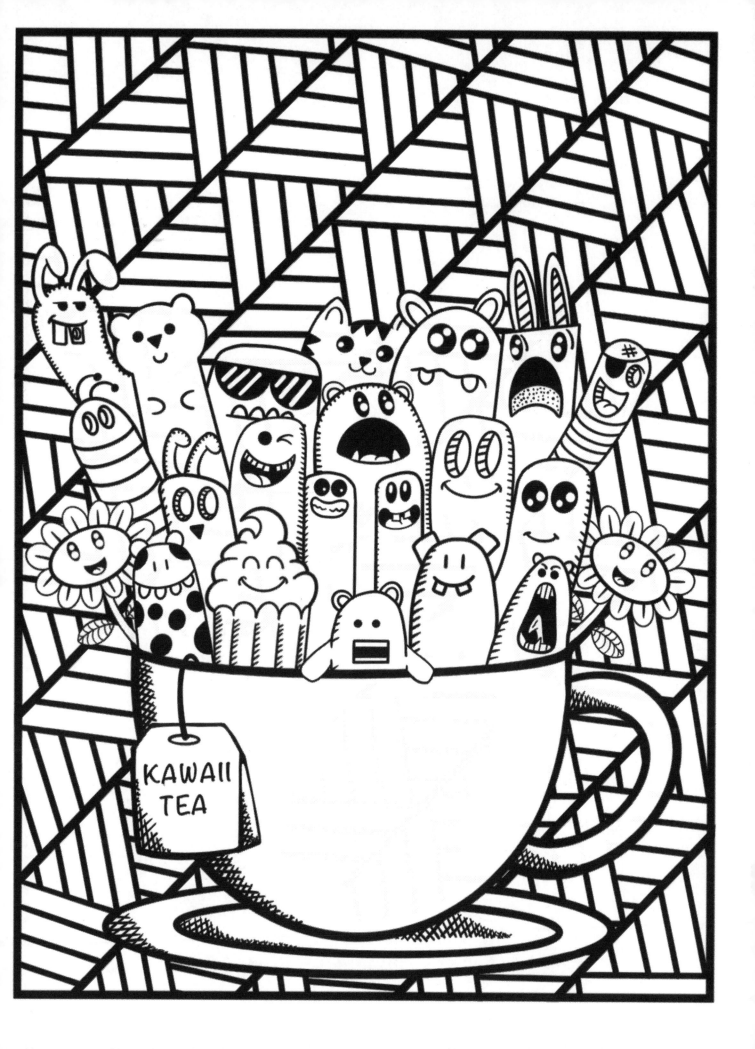

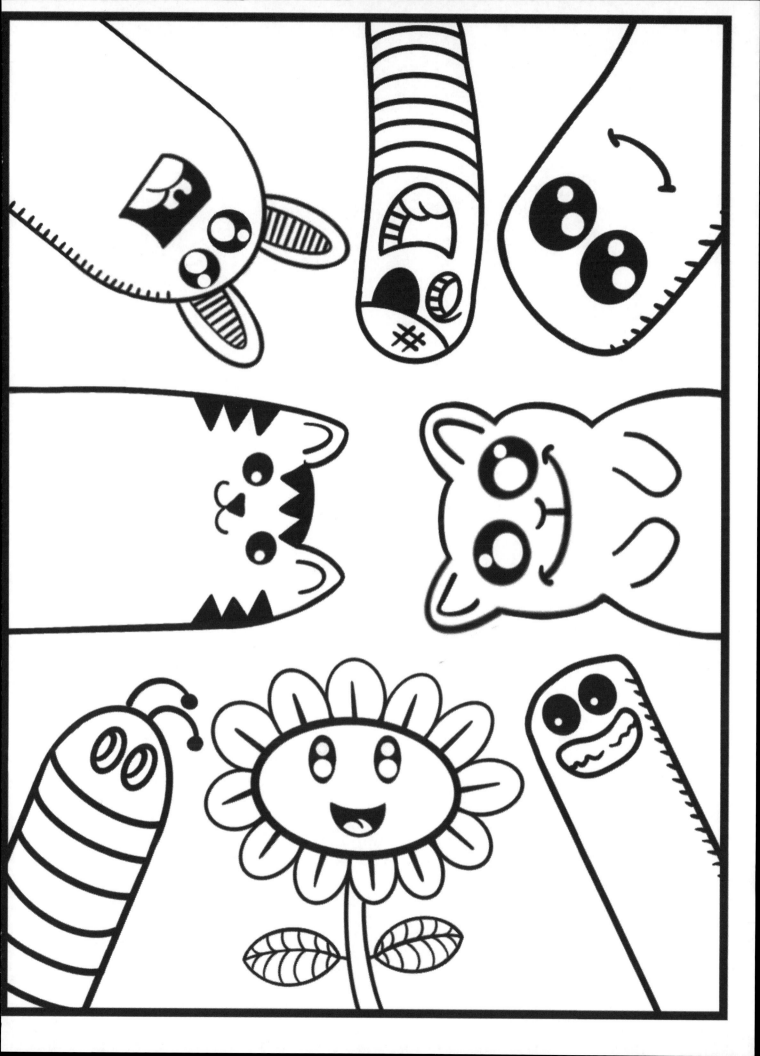

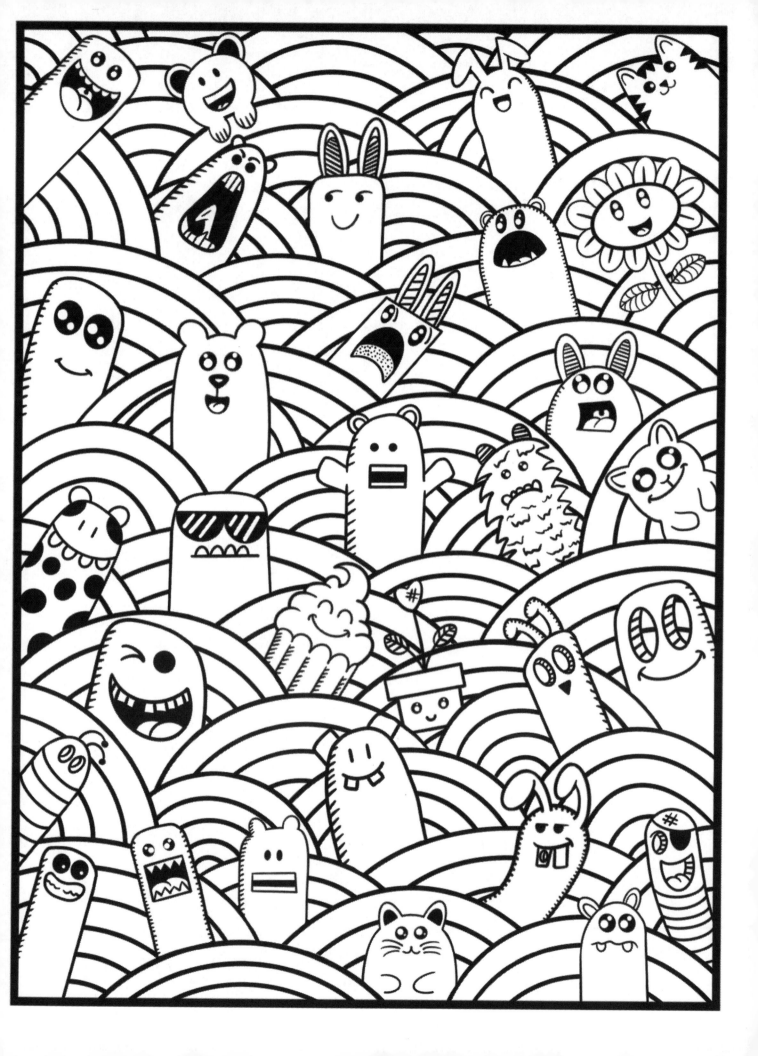

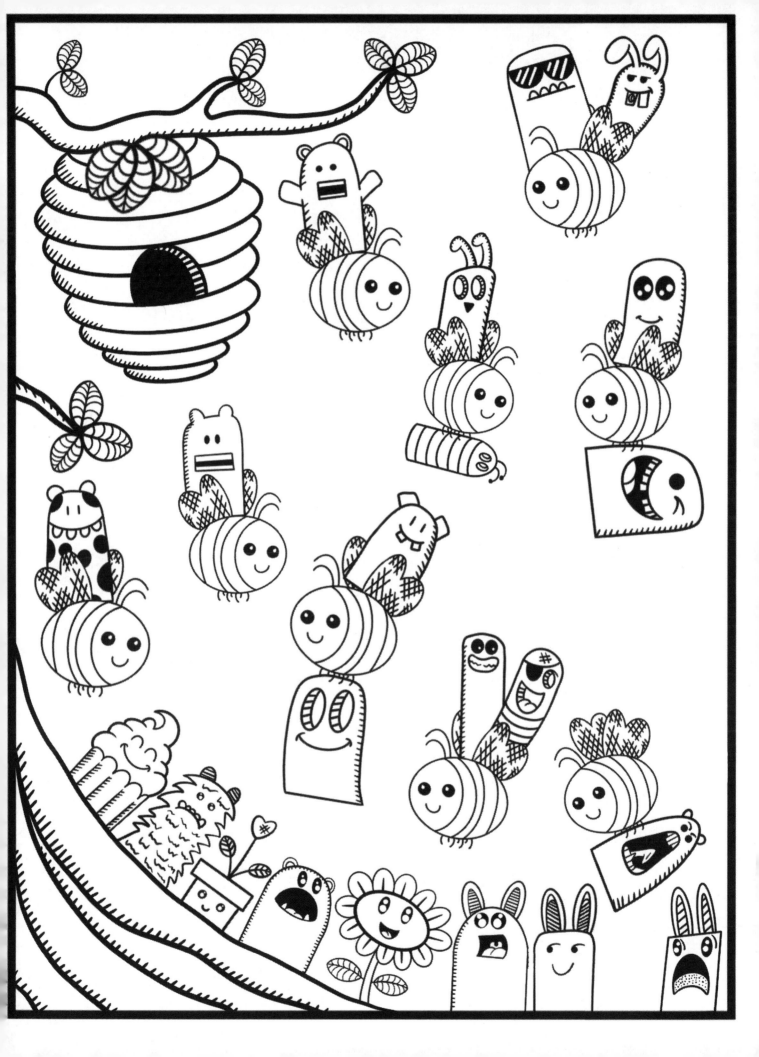

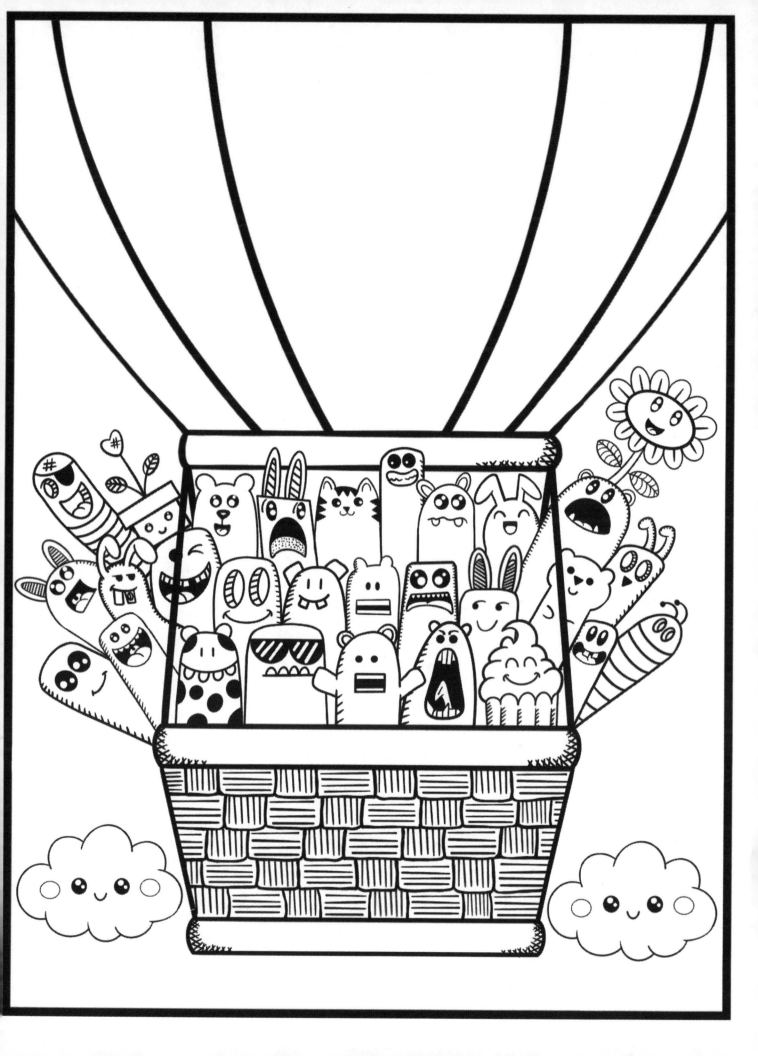

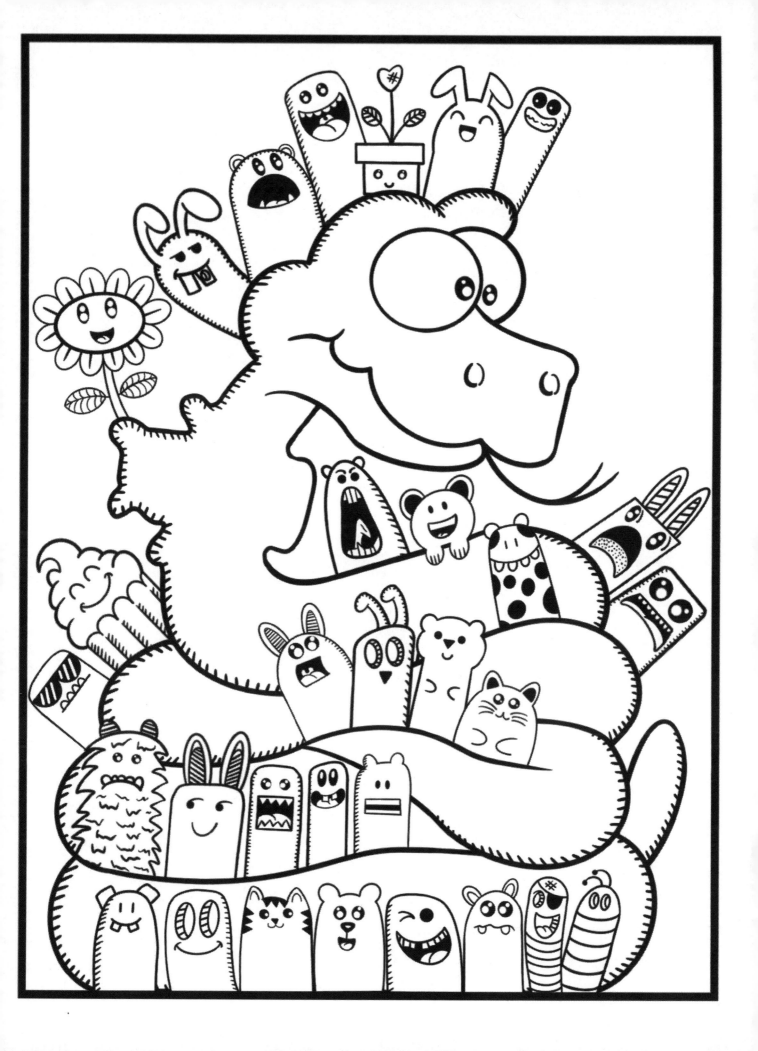

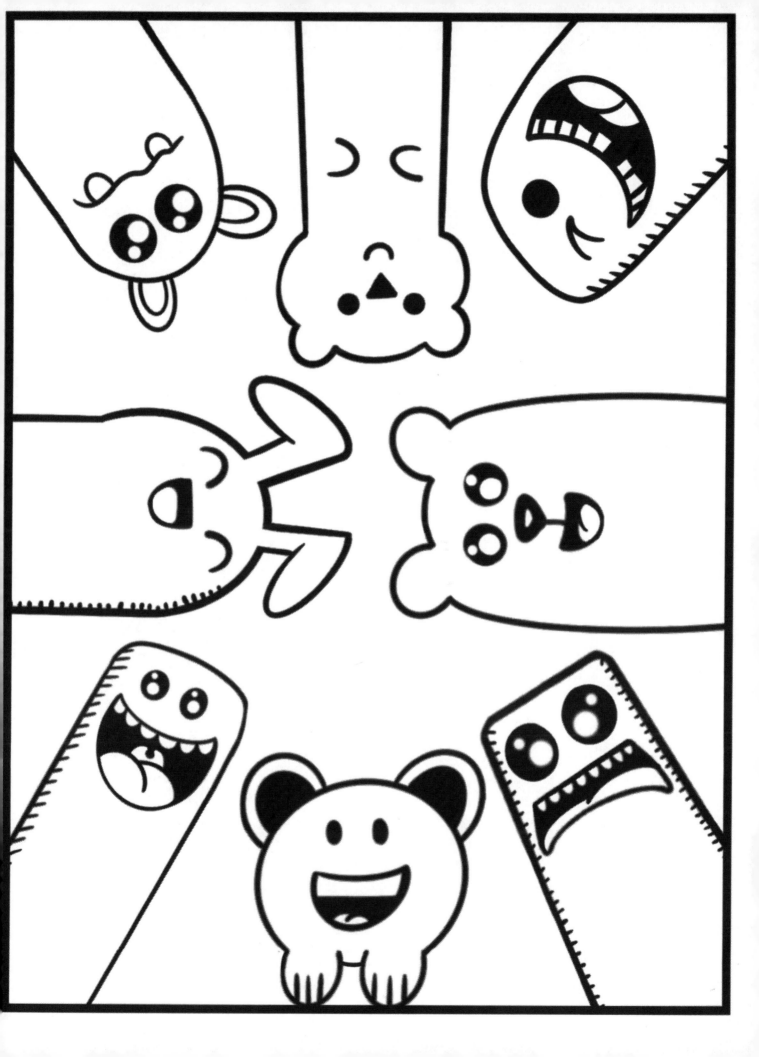

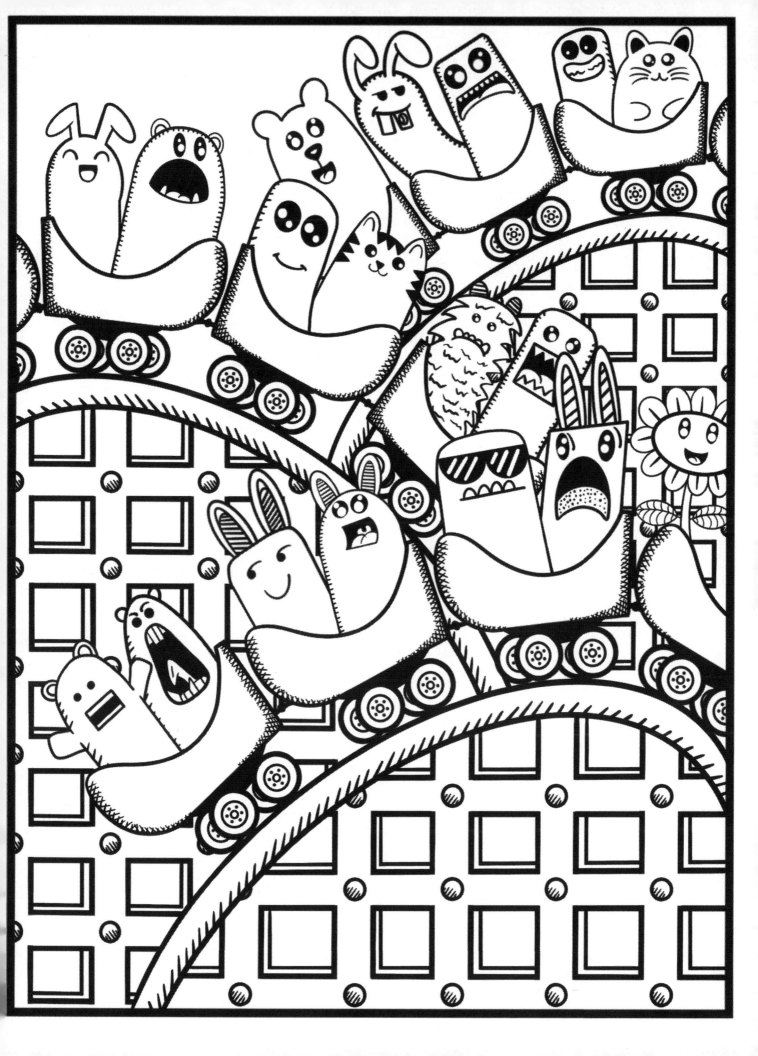

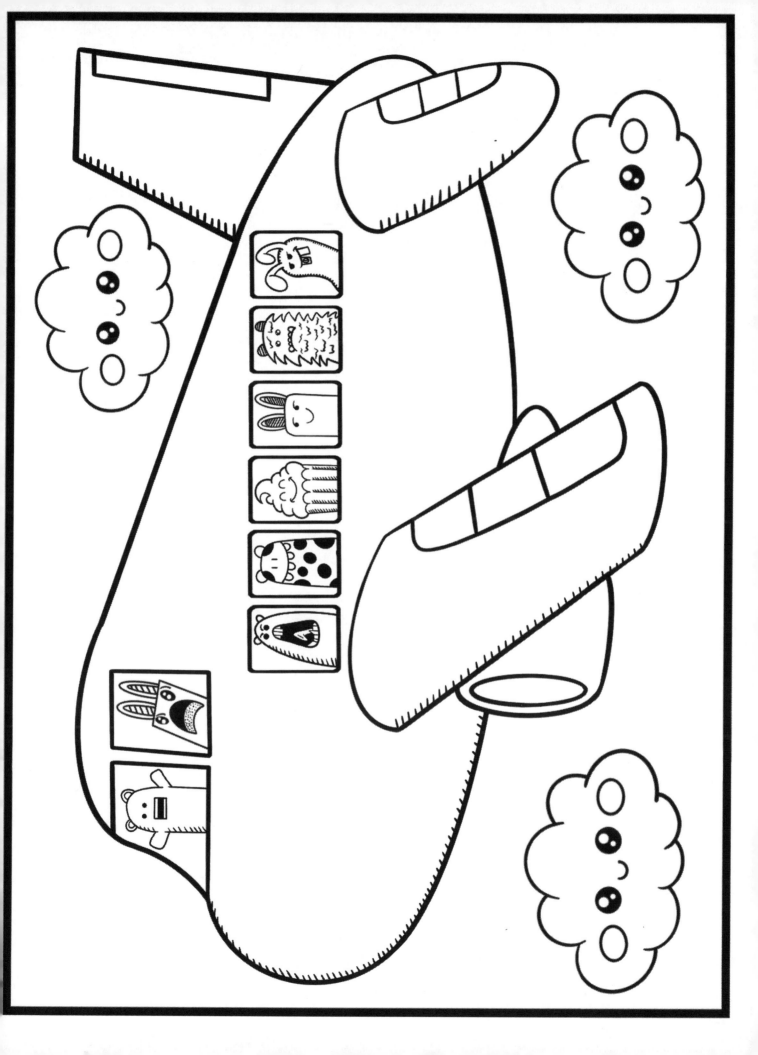

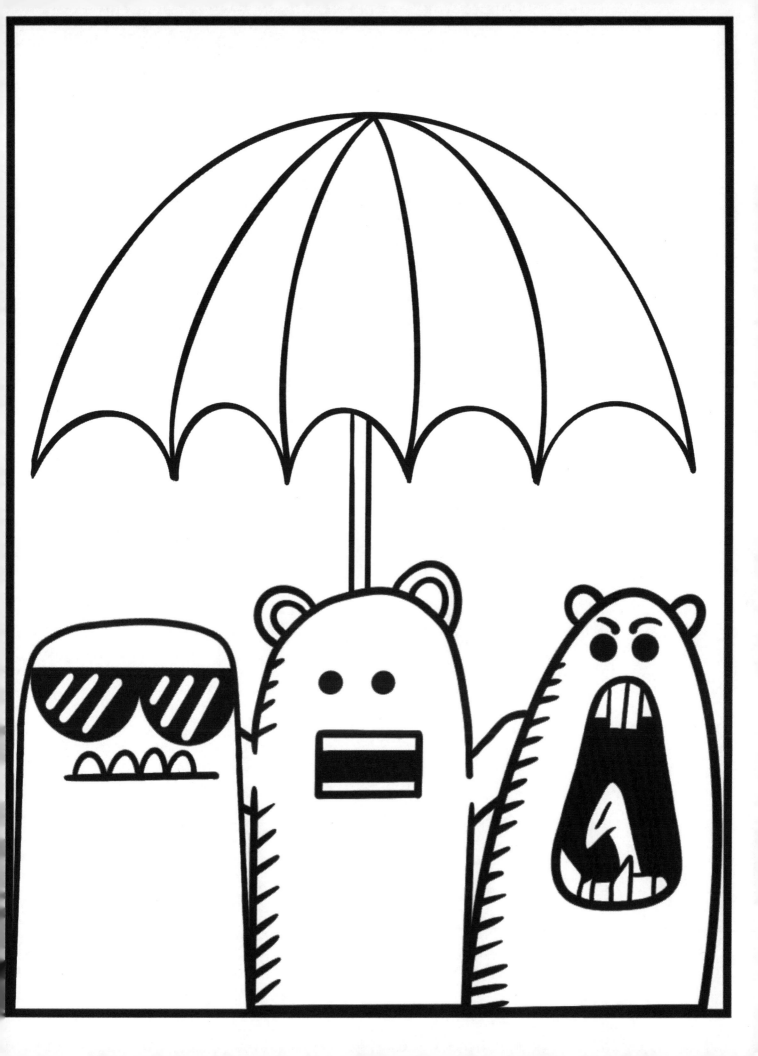

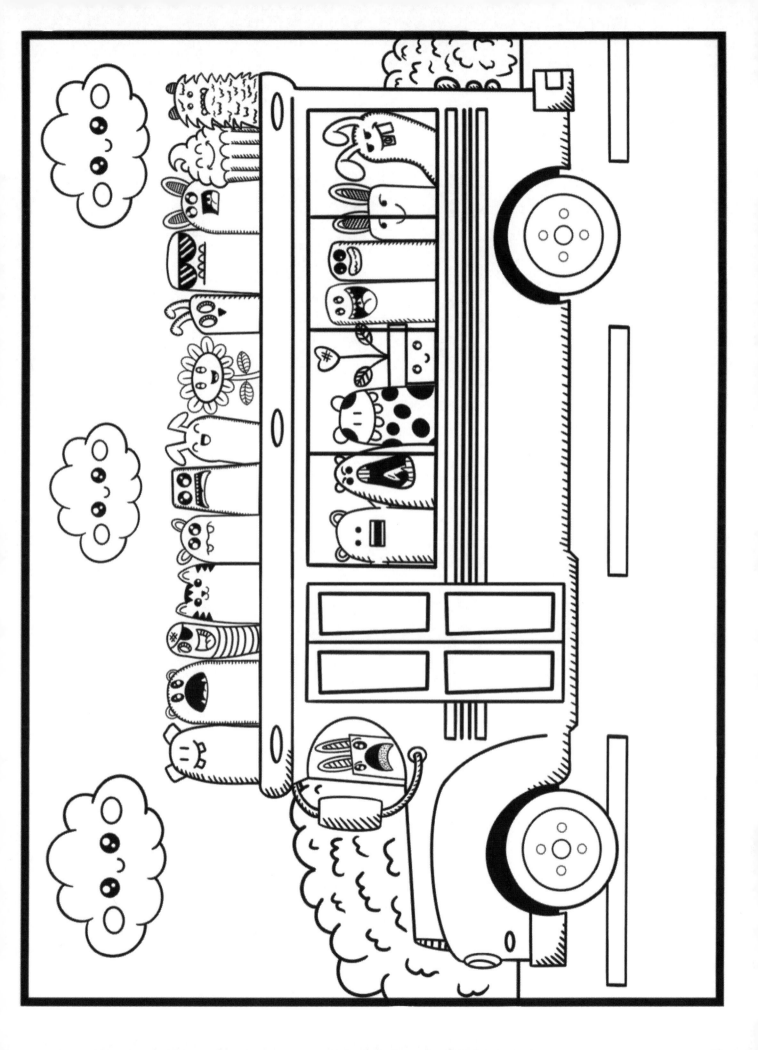

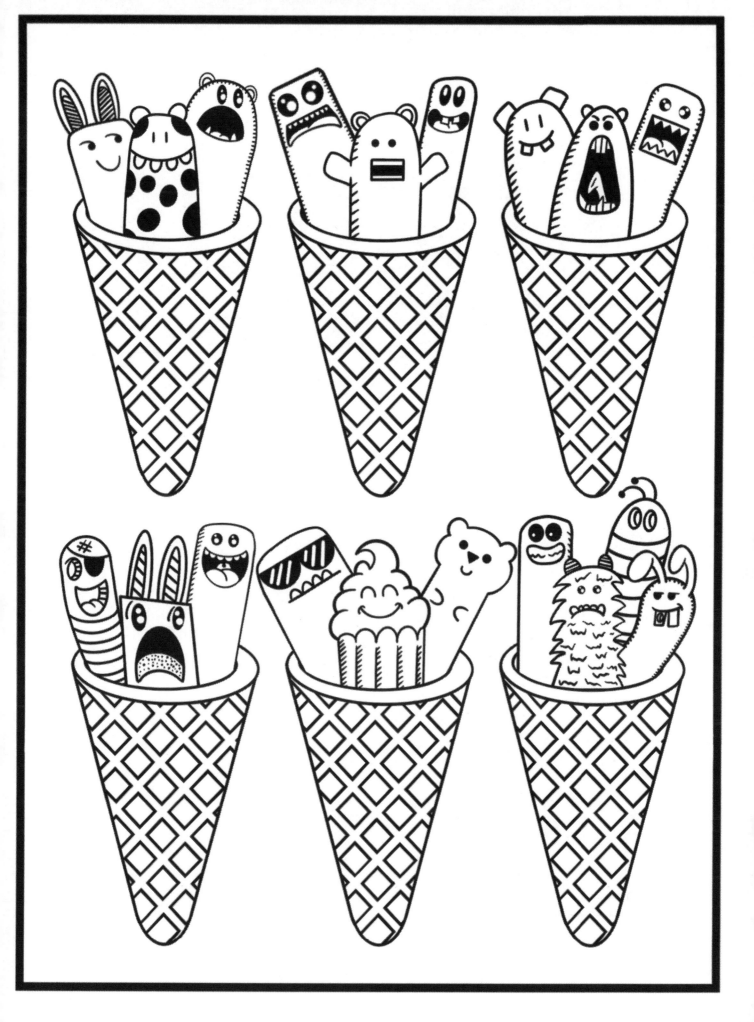

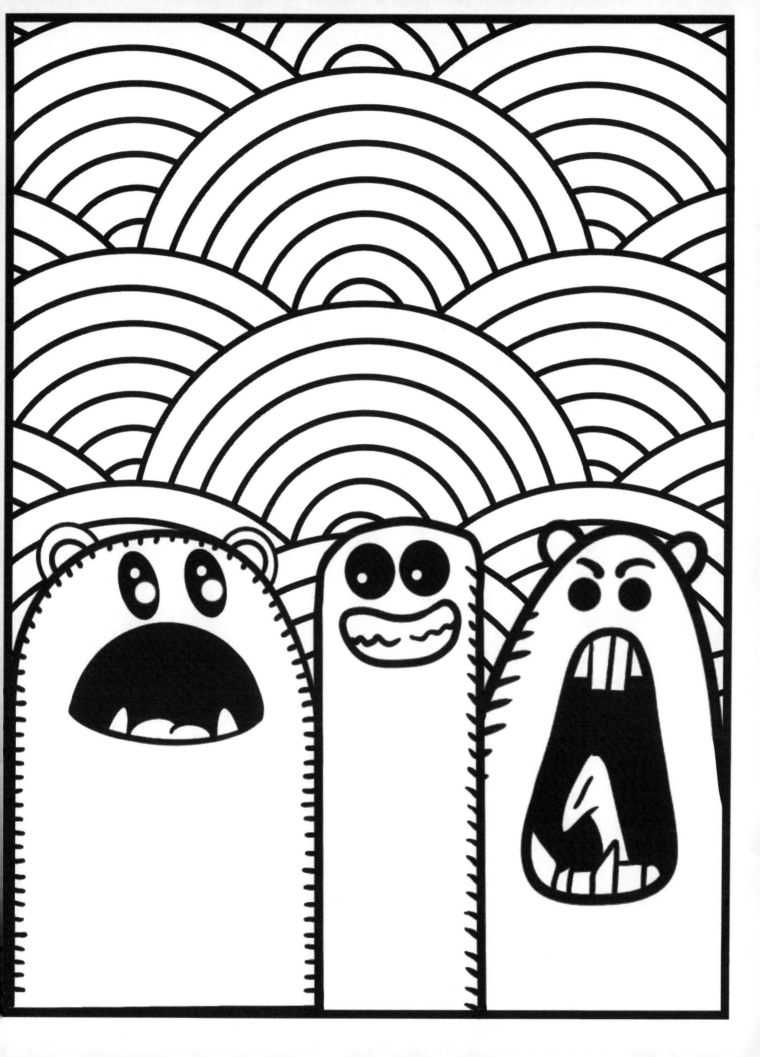

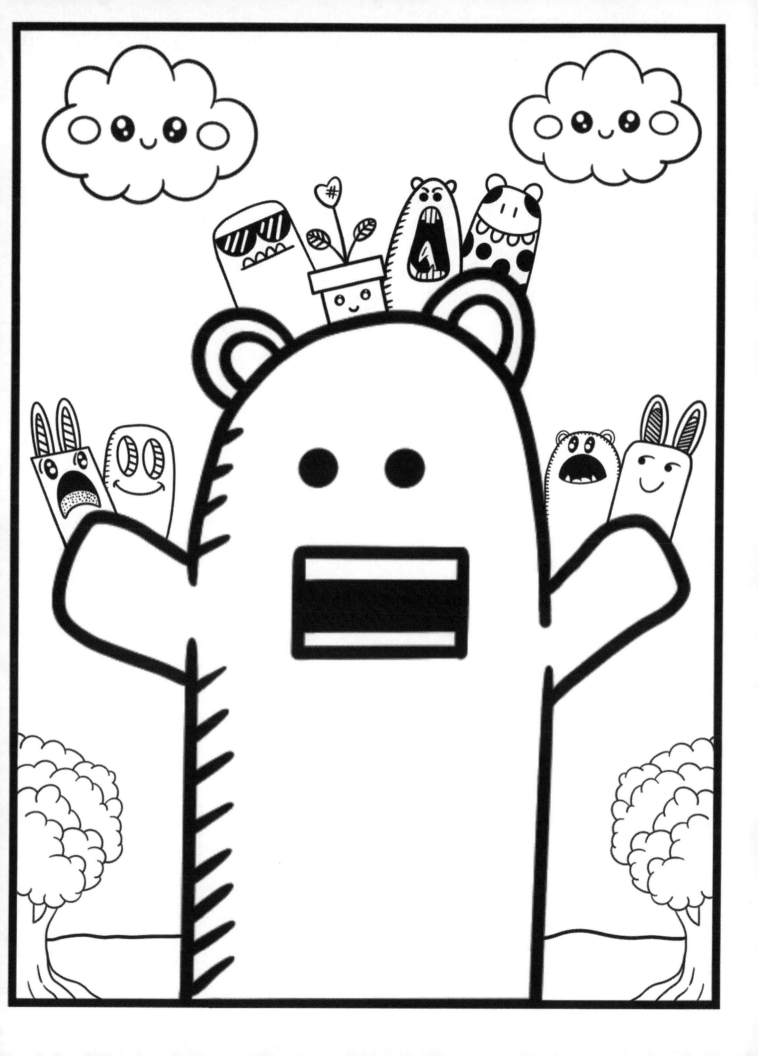

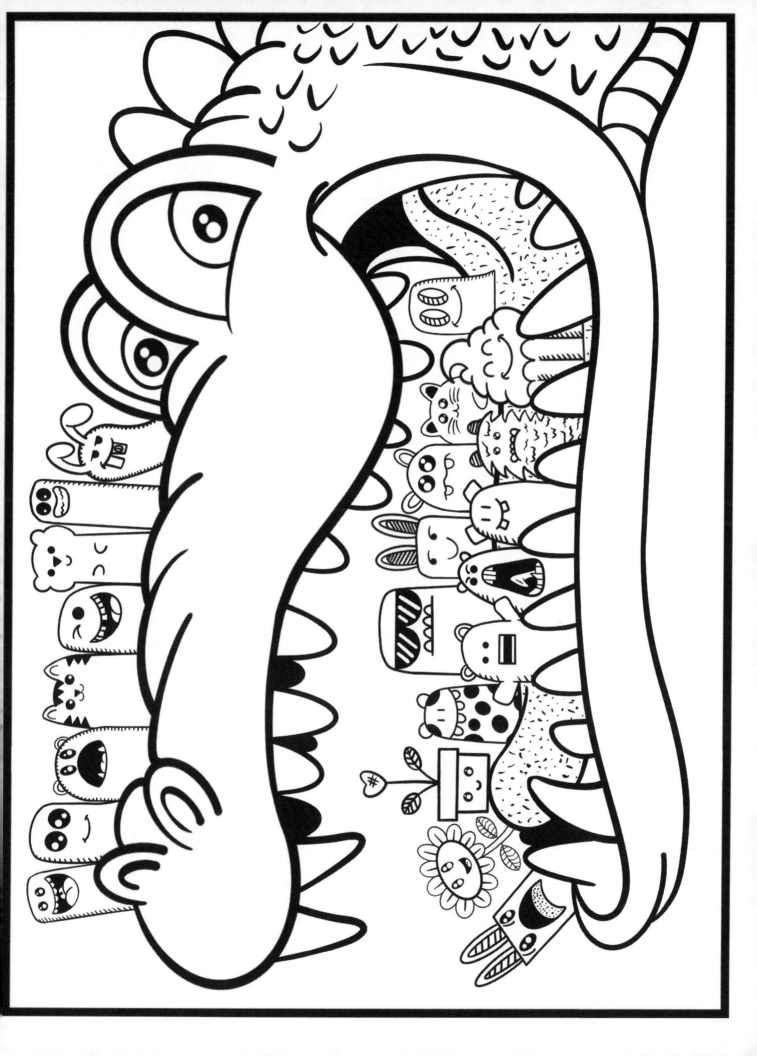

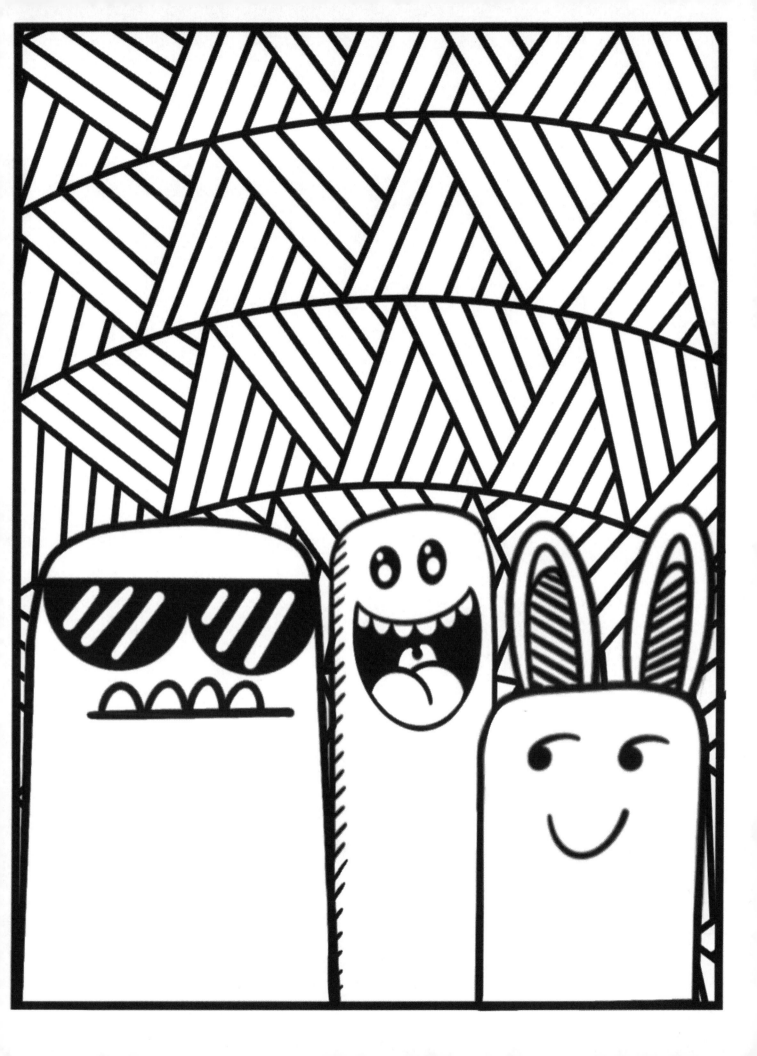

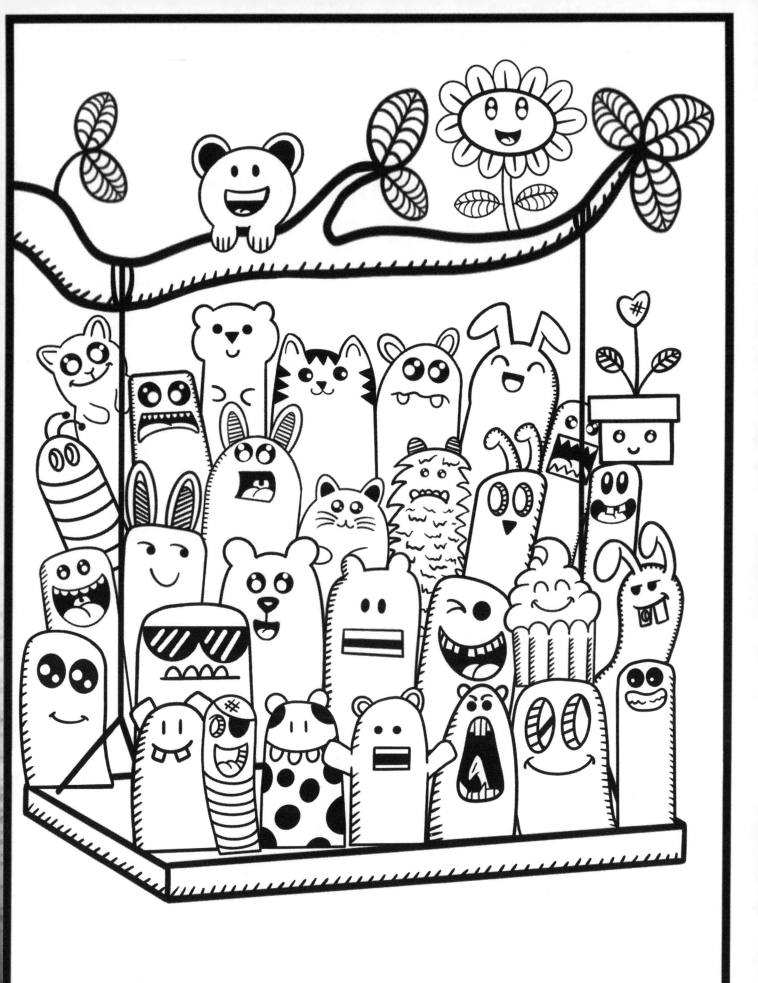

Made in the USA
Columbia, SC
01 April 2022

58387570R00035